Including pupils with Autism
at break and lunchtimes

SALLY HEWITT

A NASEN Publication

Published in 2003

ISBN 1 901485 57 9

Published by NASEN.
NASEN is a registered charity. Charity No. 1007023.
NASEN is a company limited by guarantee, registered in England and Wales.
Company No. 2637438.

Further copies of this book and details of NASEN's many other publications may be obtained from the NASEN Bookshop at its registered office:
NASEN House, 4/5 Amber Business Village, Amber Close, Amington, Tamworth, Staffs. B77 4RP.
Tel: 01827 311500; Fax: 01827 313005; Email: welcome@nasen.org.uk
Website: www.nasen.org.uk

Copy editing by Kirsten Westaway
Cover design by Mark Procter
Typeset in Times by J. C. Typesetting and printed in the United Kingdom by Stowes, Stoke-on-Trent.

Including pupils with Autism at break and lunchtimes

Contents

Acknowledgements

With thanks to Julie Crate, Charlie Henry, Chris Nichols, Sandra Fisher, Annette Clarke, Sue Sengupta, Tessa Knott, David Clayton-Evans and the many staff, parents and pupils I've been privileged to work with.

Also with special thanks to Sam, Will, Hannah and Lillie and my parents and Downham Market Christian Fellowship for supporting me in this venture.

3

Including pupils with Autism
at break and lunchtimes

Foreword

*'Undoubtedly there are all sorts of languages in the world,
yet none of them is without meaning. If then I do not grasp
the meaning of what someone is saying, I am a foreigner
to the speaker and he is a foreigner to me.'*

(1 Corinthians 14)

Including pupils with Autism
at break and lunchtimes

Introduction

Many children with autism are being educated in mainstream schools nowadays. With no easy visible signs of having the disorder, many of these children sadly become ostracised by their peers, especially at play and during lunchtimes.

There should be no doubt that all break and midday supervisory staff have an important role to play in the progressive mainstream education of pupils with autism. For reasons examined in this booklet playtimes and lunchtimes are notoriously difficult for some pupils to cope with. Because specialist, adapted approaches need to be used, inclusively operating schools ensure all involved staff, including Midday Supervisory Assistants (MSA's), are aware of those pupils with autism under their supervision.

Some teachers and classroom support assistants undergo specialist training in autism. This may or may not extend to include break and lunchtime supervision strategies. This booklet allows all supervisory staff easy access to important information (particularly relating to play and lunchtimes), also specialist approaches to use during those times.

Because pupils derive most aid when *all* involved work together to help support them, other staff members may also derive benefit from contained information.

'Children with autism exhibit, to a greater or lesser degree, a Triad of Impairment which is the defining characteristic of autism.

Communication – language impairment across all modes of communication, speech, intonation, facial expression and other body language.

Imagination – rigidity and inflexibility of thought process, resistance to change, obsessive and ritualistic behaviour.

Socialisation – difficulties with social relationships, poor social timing, lack of social empathy, rejection of normal body contact, inappropriate eye contact.'
(Dr. Lorna Wing)

A history of autism
(including Asperger Syndrome)

Leo Kanner, a child psychiatrist in Boston USA studied a group of children whose behaviour he reported in 1943 as being 'markedly and uniquely different' to that of most others. Unlike the majority of children, these children preferred to focus on objects rather than other people. Many of these children couldn't speak whilst others had an obvious delay in language acquisition. Those that did speak didn't seem to understand the importance of, or possess the skill of appropriate communicative exchange. Some of these children were able to recall past events in precise sequenced detail. These children typically became anxious and upset if anything changed. All appeared physically normal. Each displayed a distinct preferred withdrawal or 'profound autistic aloneness'.

The following year, 1944, **Hans Asperger**, a paediatrician living and working in Vienna wrote about another group of children. Their behaviour was also different to most others. These children all had average or above average IQ's. They frequently had obsessive or unusual interests. Whilst these children could all speak fluently none seemed to understand the importance of, or basic rules of appropriate communicative exchange. Despite good articulation and vocabulary content individuals spoke in a monotone, formal or pedantic way. The children in this group made attempts at joining in and mixing with others but on doing so, typically got it wrong. Many were ill co-ordinate. The children in this group became upset and anxious if anything changed. Individuals aware of being different became noticeably depressed.

In 1979 **Wing and Gould** published a study of a group of individuals they had carried out in Camberwell. Similarly to Kanner and Asperger's groups this group also displayed certain common difficulties. These were identified as being in the three skills of *socialisation*, *communication* and *imagination* - now collectively referred to as the **Triad of Impairments** – and which became the basis of diagnosis.

Following Wing & Gould's study a further theory, that of people with autism having no 'Theory of mind' – ie: an inability to understand other people's mental states - was developed by Uta Frith, Simon Baron-Cohen and Alan Leslie. Since then, much research has and still is being done regarding all aspects of the disorder.

Because no two individuals are affected in exactly the same way or to the same degree, it was decided to refer to each one as having an autistic spectrum disorder (ASD). Because of the noticeable differences between the two groups it was further decided to record some as having Asperger Syndrome. Asperger Syndrome individuals typically:

- Display odd or inappropriate social approaches

- Have ability to speak fluently, often using complicated words

- Speak in a pedantic way

- May speak in formal, mono or otherwise stilted tone

- Possess average or above average IQ

- Have awareness of being 'different'

- Are prone to literal interpretations

- May be prone to low self-esteem

- Appear ill co-ordinate

- Have unusual and/or obsessive interests

- Display flapping or twizzling of hands/objects

Those individuals with more typical autism commonly display:

- A preferred withdrawal from others

- Preference to focus on objects rather than people

- Delayed, failed or otherwise impaired language acquisition

- Over sensitivity to environmental stimuli

- Good cognitive potential

- Desire for repetitive and stereotyped play

- Extreme anxiety or reluctance to change

What causes autism?

There is widespread and much publicised theory relating to the cause of autism. Some suggest it is a genetic disorder, running in families like build and height etc. Others, a metabolic disorder with difficulties arising from the way chemicals are processed in the body. Still others suggest that autism is caused by brain injuries resulting from traumatic or premature births. The most recent, highly controversial theory is it may be as a result of the MMR injection.

However, despite these theories and ongoing research it seems reasonable to report that to date there is no fully conclusive evidence about the causes of autism and no 'miracle cure'.

Most sensible present day research suggests that whatever the cause, autism can be managed with applied specialist effort.

The long term effects of autism

Many people with autism (just like many people without it) mature to lead happy, successful lives. Some may require sheltered or residential housing accommodation whilst others are able to live quite independently. Some may work or get married or not. Some people go on to higher education, achieving diplomas and degrees. Just like the rest of us, the lives of adults with autism vary enormously from person to person.

The frequency and diagnosis of autism

Autism is a medical disorder that affects approximately 4 times more boys than girls. About ten times more boys than girls are affected by Asperger Syndrome.

To be diagnosed as having ASD a child (or adult) will display combined difficulties in the skills of *communication, socialisation* and *imagination* (the triad of impairments as earlier defined by Dr. Lorna Wing). Doctors or community paediatricians are commonly those responsible for recording and making an official diagnosis. This will be after extensive study of the individual together with collating relevant information from parents, schools and other involved professionals. These professionals may include:

Educational psychologists (EP's) – provide support to help children with difficulties in school settings.

Clinical psychologists (CP's) - provide support to help children with difficulties outside of school.

Speech & language therapists – provide support to help children with difficulties in communication.

The fact we have access to a great deal of information about autism now means it is often diagnosed quite early. This is seen as a positive thing by parents and schools.

More typical autism (as most easily identified in Kanner's study group) can be diagnosed as early as about 18 months old although the most common diagnostic age is 2-3 years old.

Asperger Syndrome is usually diagnosed at about 4-5 years old, although it has been known to come as late as 30 years old. Older, more able individuals frequently report a sense of relief at finally receiving diagnosis (and therefore more widely accepted recognition) of their difficulties. Some individuals are never 'officially' diagnosed but may be referred to as having or displaying tendencies or behaviour 'commonly associated with' ASD.

Whilst it would be foolish to consider any individual as being 'a little bit autistic', there are infinite varying degrees of autism contained on the spectrum. It is also believed by some that we are *all* on the spectrum somewhere.

Common playground
and lunchtime behaviours

Understanding the triad of impairments helps to give a better and real understanding of the difficulties pupils face at play and lunchtimes.

'Communication – language impairment across all modes of communication, speech, intonation, facial expression and other body language.'

The skill of effective social communication is a complex, intricate one. Not only do we use our voices, we also use body language, gesture, intonation (the way we say something), facial expression, prosody (volume and speed of speech) and eye contact as well. Sometimes we don't have to hear or say anything at all to know what a person is trying to communicate (to us). We can tell a lot by a frown, smile or stance. Pointing is another important part of communication. As babies and toddlers, even if we don't know or can't say the words, most of us quickly learn to point to what we want. Most of us are easily able, just by looking and listening, to gather what another person is really trying to tell us. We can easily pick up on jokes, inference, importance or moods.

Communication impairment frequently results in children with ASD being prevented from naturally doing, understanding *and appropriately responding* to all these things.

For example, a (excitedly) raised voice to a child with ASD will have no obvious effect except perhaps to encourage him or her to shout back even louder. In extreme cases it may frighten the child to the degree that in future he refuses to even acknowledge his own name. Likewise, asking a child "Do you want to/Shall we?" invariably elicits a "Yes/No" reply rather than one which shows understanding of the inferred meaning.

When we consider the many and diverse ways school children communicate - especially during play and lunchtimes - we begin to understand how challenging these times may be for pupils with ASD. The *most* effective social communication also relies on the natural ability to adapt it to suit any given new social situation and setting in a way that ASD pupils find extremely challenging.

'Imagination – rigidity and inflexibility of thought process, resistance to change, obsessive and ritualistic behaviour.'

When applied to changing or new social situations and settings, the skill of imagination is a powerful tool. The majority of us instinctively use it to help avert and manage potentially embarrassing, threatening, dangerous or otherwise 'frightening' times. Many of us (learn to) thrive on change, naturally rising to the social, behavioural and academic learning pressures and challenges each new situation and setting brings.

Imagination impairment makes it difficult for individuals with ASD to naturally read and react appropriately to new or different social settings. Rigid, inflexible thought processes prevent easy transference of learnt skills. For example, although a child may have learned an appropriate social behaviour or approach at home or in the classroom, he or she will not necessarily know to adapt and/or apply this in the playground or dining hall unless this has been specifically taught.

A natural resistance to any change may cause a child to become anxious or upset. Individuals commonly display self-comforting behaviours during times of distress or confusion. These behaviours are often obsessive and ritualistic and may include (whole body) rocking, (hand) flapping or other repeated movement, or running up and down or around playground boundaries. Unusual verbal repeats – humming, muttering etc – are also possibilities.

Another consequence of imagination impairment restricts a child's ability to pretend or otherwise imaginatively play – something the majority of other children do regularly.

When we consider the countless number of different changes during any one single play or lunchtime we start to see how demanding these times may be for children with ASD.

'Socialisation – difficulties with social relationships, poor social timing, lack of social empathy, rejection of normal body contact, inappropriate eye contact.'

During playtime the majority of younger children in particular are natural social butterflies, happily flitting from child to child, group to group. As they do so, they quickly learn and apply all the unwritten social cues and rules that abound. If they make a mistake they usually quickly learn from it. As they become older they begin to form closer friendships with one or two others, also retaining knowledge and participation of the much wider circle.

Good social skills allow observation and provision of what type of approaches to apply to others in any given situation. Most people instinctively adapt their approaches to support another who is upset or hurt. This may include sympathetic verbal, eye and body contact. Depending on the situation, it may also incorporate keeping a distance.

Socialisation impairment typically affects an individual's understanding and therefore appropriate response to all these things.

For those who much prefer to withdraw from others, play and lunchtimes are wholly contrary to their instinctive need and natural preference. Individuals may become frightened or feel threatened. When frightened or threatened they commonly resort to unusual self-comforting, obsessive behaviours. This can often result in them being bullied or teased.

For those with Asperger Syndrome who desperately want to join in but typically make repeated mistakes, lunch and playtimes can quickly become less enjoyable. Always making mistakes can lead to them being bullied or teased. To those prone to low self-esteem at the best of times, this may lead to depression. In extreme cases, even young children with Asperger Syndrome talk about suicide.

In conclusion, triad impairments naturally prevent children with ASD independently enjoying and deriving full benefit from play and lunchtimes. By discreetly applying specialist approaches, informed supervising adults can work to help support pupils. Some approaches may initially require extra staff vigilance and repeated physical application. However, as pupils become more confident and able, this may be tactfully backward chained to provide a level of support more in line with others.

Individual pupils have differing play and lunchtime needs – indoor playtimes, outdoor playtimes and dining hall. To help you find the approach you need quickly and easily the following section has been divided into three parts. Many of the strategies are interchangeable and/or easily adapted to suit each different environment.

But first of all, the next section includes some useful general approaches. Many of these approaches can be useful when tackling any challenging behaviour and can avoid singling an individual out. Specific examples in this and the other three parts have been detailed although names, where used, have been changed.

ASD specialist approaches
(useful, general)

- **A pupil may not be aware the word 'everybody' includes him, therefore personally addressing him or her by name in any group situation will assist in this understanding.** *Telling a child the word 'everybody' includes him or her also helps. (Situations may include dining hall prayer time, line-ups, tidy time, end of playtime etc. Pupils often tend to 'opt out' of those situations they do not particularly enjoy or cannot easily make sense of.*

A primary pupil with AS daily ignored all general requests of 'Everybody hands together/eyes closed for prayer time' in the dining hall, preferring instead to flap his hands (ie. effectively 'switching himself off' from what was going on around him) until it was over. His obviously different behaviour during this time often attracted unkind comments and peer displays of mimicking behaviour. When staff added a repetition of "Sean. The word everybody includes you" the pupil, recognising his name, stopped flapping his hands thus removing the barrier between himself and others. Staff were then able to continue to direct him (and others they also later successfully used this technique with) to joining in.

- **Whatever their intellectual ability, autistic thought processes typically prevent easy processing of large quantities of verbal language.** *Keeping instructions simple, minimal and direct will help a pupil understand your exact requirements. Allowing an extra few seconds of 'processing' time is also useful. (Whenever expected to co-operate to given task/activity).*

School was experiencing difficulties in encouraging a pupil to return and properly clear his finished dinner tray (ie. Scrape off, put cutlery in relevant tubs, stack glass etc). The only part of the original lengthy instruction the pupil actually complied with before making his quick exit was taking his tray up (to the trolley).
By:

1. Breaking the instruction into smaller stages, ie: "David. Take your tray to the trolley **then** scrape the food off **then** I'll tell you what to do next" and

2. Using pointing gestures and initial physical guidance at each stage, staff eventually elicited a satisfactory response.

By initially allowing David time to thought process even the most simple of verbal instruction eg. "Now stack your glass" **before actually expecting him to do it** staff relieved the pressure on David to 'do' and 'think it through to make sure I get it right' at the same time. As David became more confident in getting each stage right, staff discreetly withdrew support (which initially included ample verbal praise) to enable his ultimate independence and inclusive performance of this task.

- **Whenever it is necessary to repeat a given instruction, using the exact wording again will avoid potentially confusing and/or distressing situations.** *Changing even one word may result in the pupil interpreting it as an entirely different request altogether. (Whenever pupil doesn't respond after the first time).*

School was having difficulties encouraging a nursery pupil to help during tidy times. On being told "Jayne. Put the ball away" together with the staff use of a pointing gesture to indicate where, the little girl took the ball, looked to the toy-box (the correct place for the ball) but made no immediately obvious physical attempt to move towards it. Staff, assuming Jayne hadn't heard or simply wasn't going to do it (she was far more likely to be 'thought processing') then said "Jayne. Put the ball up" to which Jayne responded by throwing it into the air. When later using exact same word repeats and processing time, staff encouraged Jayne's co-operation.

- **For those individuals commonly prone to literal interpretations, offering even the smallest of choices may elicit an inappropriate response or reply.** *Keeping all instructional language direct and most specific in requirements cajoles better pupil response. (Particularly relevant to those individuals with Asperger Syndrome. Eg. avoid telling a child to eat 'just a little bit more' when you actually mean him to eat lot more. Avoid asking 'do you want to line up now?' when you mean 'line up now' etc).*

A group of MSA's voiced concerns of an AS pupil who, during a 'normal' lunchtime would make up to a dozen visits to show staff how much (in reality, how little) he had eaten of his main course. When I asked their responses to this all admitted to telling him, each time, to go back to his seat and eat 'just a little bit more...'. Well, he'd certainly been doing exactly as he'd been told and at least staff approach was consistent! When later using more specific instructions and initially physically dividing food on his plate to indicate precisely how much more, the pupil soon developed greater awareness of true expectations.

Many schools have difficulty in getting children to line up, at the end of playtimes for example. When considering that besides inferred instructions, (eg. Do you? Will you?) being used, phrases such as "Go to the **back** of the line" or "**Join** the line" or "**Get in** the line" are also used it becomes apparent how confusing these might be for those prone to literal interpretation. A simple and direct "Tim. Line up now" together with initial physical guidance and pointing etc if necessary, is more widely understood and effective.

- **Some individuals may be extremely cunning in manipulating withdrawal or 1-1 adult attention by using displays of inappropriate behaviour.** *Focusing on and praising positives, no matter how small, or 'naturally expected' or, briefly displayed will work to avoid unintentionally encouraging this. (Specific positives may include good sitting, walking, eating, sharing, waiting etc).*

Mark's messy eating and general table manners were causing great difficulties. Talking with his mouth full often resulted in half chewed food being sprayed onto the table and other's plates and clothes, also, on one occasion, Mark almost choking. Kneeling up on the chair, Mark often knocked others drinks over. After the choking incident, Mark was withdrawn from the dining hall to sit on a chair outside it, given a glass of water and supervised 1-1. During this time out, Mark's parents were called and informed of the incident. They responded by going up to school to see him. By the time his parents arrived, Mark was chatting happily to the supervising member of staff and of course, was delighted to see his parents. The next day, Mark 'choked' again (although this time staff noted the choking actually appeared more a bout of bad coughing) but, as a precaution he was again withdrawn from the dining hall for 1-1 supervision. And so a pattern was set. Mark quickly learned that although spitting food, knocking others drinks over, and even fidgeting in his chair were not rewarded by positive adult attention, 'choking' in the dining hall was. As soon as staff began to praise Mark for his (initially fleeting) positive behaviours in the dining hall (good sitting, eating, waiting etc) the coughing bouts, to all intents and purposes, stopped. In the event he did begin 'choking' staff,

15

although keeping a careful distance watch would not approach him to praise on another positive until after he had stopped. In this way, Mark soon learned his negative behaviours did not warrant positive staff attention.

- **Natural expectation of good pupil behaviour, particularly in any new situations or setting should never be assumed as independently forthcoming.** *Remaining constantly aware of this can avoid potentially distressing or otherwise unwanted outcomes. (Different seating or line up arrangements, introduction of new staff, game sharing expectation etc).*

During her first two terms at primary Vanessa, a classically autistic pupil had packed lunches. School policy dictated that children with packed lunches sit at different tables to those having school dinners. For the third term, Vanessa was booked for school dinners. Naturally unaware of different seating arrangements, Vanessa took her old seat at her packed lunch table. A member of staff, on noticing that Vanessa appeared to have forgotten her packed lunch, went in search of it for her. In the meantime, those having school dinners were called for their food. Vanessa was becoming increasingly agitated and disruptive. By the time school eventually discovered the little girl was booked for school dinners she was very distraught, as were staff and several other children. This situation could easily have been avoided by improved classroom/supervisory staff communication, or initially providing Vanessa with a card to show dining hall staff she was booked in for school dinners, or physically supervising Vanessa on a practice run of her new lunchtime seating arrangements.

- **Because pupils respond best to a wholly consistent approach from all staff, sharing successful approaches with** *all* **involved colleagues is** *beneficial. More fully inclusively working schools acknowledge the need and provide time (or tools) for this. (A simple 'add to' list in the staff room is an easy way to begin. Subsequently more formal discussion and/or circulation of individuals lunch and playtime needs can be made).*

Some pupils appear to show preference, even favouritism of a particular member of staff. If this happens, when the going gets tough, that same member of staff is often expected to diffuse difficult situations. Whilst in the short term this may seem the most sensible approach, in the long term it can often do more harm than good. Supervisors may become disgruntled with one another. Some may quietly take a dislike to another member of staff simply because he or she cannot manage (or apparently isn't able to) the child in the same way as they can. Fearful of an unwanted response, some staff may become reluctant of acknowledging or approaching a child in a needy situation. Preferred staff absenteeism can create huge problems. I cannot count the number of times I've been into schools only to be told "You're bound to see him at his worst today. His usual helper is away..." By sharing approaches that work, difficulties such as these can be avoided.

Ensuring supervisory staff are provided with a starting notice board resource, then regular meeting and discussion time works to provide greater management consistency, and much happier break and lunchtimes.

From experience, (and often contrary to SENCO and Head Teacher's own original thoughts!) all MSA's I've ever worked with have been prepared to work an extra hour or so per half term in order to help make this possible. Most importantly, all have been appreciative of the opportunity to understand (more) about the break and lunchtime ways of pupils with autism and approaches to use.

Experience again shows what a currently underused, under estimated resource MSA's generally are in the mainstream education of pupils with autism. As far as many pupils are concerned, break and lunchtimes are the only times they actually really look forward to at school. The fact *those times* go wrong too only adds to the mainstream pressures evidently already on pupils.

- **Forewarning pupils of any change allows 'safe' mental processing of the impending change before actually having to respond to it.** *(Indoor/outdoor/end of play/particular activity etc) For some pupils this could be a verbal or visual prompt such as a 'change' card or an egg timer. For those pupils who prefer outside play suddenly being told (even as they're putting on their coat) that there's been a change of plan, staff may suddenly find themselves with an inconsolably sobbing or unusually aggressive pupil.*

One little boy spent several agonising minutes slapping and kicking the unfortunate member of staff who divulged just such untimely information. He was eventually calmed by the promise of being able to play 'What's the time Mr. Wolf?' (his favourite outdoor activity) in the hall after it had been cleared. By verbally forewarning the pupil the next time it was necessary, this time as he was still eating his lunch, staff were better equipped (reminding him of being able to play Mr. Wolf when the hall was cleared) to mentally prepare the pupil for an enjoyable indoor playtime. As far as this particular pupil was concerned, it was not the location that bothered him but the activity he cared about. This time, and to fill the time the hall was being cleared (discreetly using 'Mr. Wolf' as an incentive/reward) staff encouraged him to join in with a card game with two other children first, thus also helping in his sharing and waiting skills etc. As similar good memories of indoor playtimes were built up and used as reminders, the pupil's reluctance and protest to this kind of unexpected change disappeared.

- **Some individuals experience cyclical mood swings described (by Dr. Tony Attwood) as 'uncontrollable waves' or 'tides' sweeping over them.** *If staff suspect this to be the case with an individual, keeping a simple mood diary/timetable can pinpoint most vulnerable times. Extra support and/or decreasing expectations during these times works to help pupils cope.*

School expressed concern about a highly intelligent, usually contented and hard working Yr 6 pupil with AS who, for no apparent reason simply sometimes had 'really bad days'. During these days it was difficult to focus the pupil to even his favourite classroom activities. On a really bad day the student would weep inconsolably, frequently complain of feeling useless, also be verbally and physically abusive and aggressive towards others. Break and lunchtime supervisory staff also mentioned about 'the odd bad day' for him but otherwise 'no real problems'.

When encouraged to keep a simple tick chart (photocopied weekly timetable sheets) of good and bad days, classroom and break and lunchtime supervisory staff were astonished to discover exact same patterns. When later encouraged to extend this to keeping a similar one himself (supported by parents), the boy's own tick chart confirmed findings of the other two. On some days, and for no apparent reason, he just woke up in a really bad mood.

The pattern having been discovered, all involved were far better equipped to manage those times. Classroom staff decreased expectations and increased praise of him, break and lunchtime supervisors allowed him quiet indoor 1-1 or chosen partner computer time, his relieved and dedicated parents offered even more tolerance, and the boy himself acquired a quiet acceptance and understanding that each mood swing or 'bad day' as it came to be known, would pass.

- **Because the pupil with ASD does not understand the implications, other pupils may find it easy to persuade them to use inappropriate body gesture or contact (including sexual) or bad language.** *Play* *and lunchtimes are especially vulnerable. Sympathetic teaching of specific acceptable behaviour and language may reduce the possibility and recurrence of this. Indoor playtimes provide a good opportunity for designated supervisory staff to provide a support programme discussed and agreed with the SENCO.*

Unsupervised games of 'tag' are frequently pinpointed as being times during which a pupil makes inappropriate physical contact with another. Staff modelling of acceptable places (shoulder, arm etc) and ways of contact (gentle touch by hand and call of tag) during 'practice run' games are the best way to teach this.

After complaints from another child's parents, a Yr 5 pupil with AS was temporarily excluded after an incident involving 'inappropriate sexual conduct'. It transpired this had occurred during an unsupervised game of tag. When questioned, it quickly became apparent the boy had no idea what the fuss was all about; as far as he was concerned he had tagged the girl (on her bottom, over her skirt), which meant she should have been *it*. In this case, school was extremely understanding and not only set up a SENCO agreed 'Acceptable touching' programme to assist the pupil, but supported this with modelling and greater supervision in the playground. Simple body outlines were also used to show appropriate and unacceptable (good and bad) contact points. Encouraging the pupil to keep the 'good' sheet as a reminder at the beginning of each break time was initially useful.

Some pupils with AS may be extremely prone to being easily persuaded by others to make offensive remarks. A usually polite and well-mannered student found himself in all sorts of trouble after sexually propositioning several female members of staff. It transpired that although he felt uncomfortable doing it, he didn't want to get 'beaten up' by the lads who were *telling* him to do it. In this case the pupil was encouraged, and initially every time anyone at school said anything to make him feel similarly uncomfortable, to immediately show a 'Can we talk about...?' card to staff. This gave the pupil a starting point of opportunity to discuss whether or not he should do whatever it was he felt uncomfortable about. It also allowed a quicker staff response in addressing any real bullying issues.

One of the most effective ways of eliminating the use of insulting or swear words is to encourage the pupil to help make a 'Bin list' of all those he or she uses. A primary pupil began using vast amounts of swear words. This resulted in playtime detentions, withdrawals, fraught meetings with parents and the boy's behaviour and learning process generally deteriorating. When working it through with him, staff were encouraged to help him verbalise and make a list of all the swear words and offensive phrases he used. (I had earlier forewarned staff this strategy provides no opportunity for faint heartedness!) This in itself was the real turning point; the boy actually had no idea that many of the words he had been using were swear words, or generally thought of as being unkind or offensive. It also transpired one or two others had told him to use some of them, and that he had often heard (especially during breaktimes) others using them too.

The next part of this technique was to write (but not say) individual words or phrases onto smaller pieces of paper. The final part was for the boy to screw up each piece and throw it away into the bin, thereby unable to use it ever again. It took only two more similar sessions, each involving only one word, before the boy's swearing stopped.

With these useful, general approaches in mind we now move on to the individual sections of dining hall, playground and indoor playtimes.

ASD specialist approaches in the dining hall

- **Pupils of all ages may have little or no real idea who or what role, dining hall supervisory assistants play.** *Approaching younger pupils at the beginning of each session to specifically remind them of what to do if help is needed is therefore useful (stay in seat, put up hand etc). Telling a pupil your name also helps.*

Despite quickly learning adults are there to help them in the classroom, pupils may not necessarily extend this generalisation into the dining hall. One child, desperate for the toilet during lunchtime, ran out of the hall and back into his classroom to ask his teacher's permission. By the time he (and the bemused dining hall supervisory assistant following him) found her, it was too late. The little boy soon became very reluctant to go into lunch, eventually only being persuaded by his teacher going in with him to settle him. Later, having been introduced to dining hall supervisory staff, all of whom assured him they were there to help him (including if he needed to go to the toilet) he quickly regained confidence and lunchtime independence.

Even secondary school pupils may not recognise supervisory assistants as being there to help. Initially introducing new pupils (before lunchtime if possible) to supervisory staff, goes a long way to assisting in their more confident participation. A more fully inclusive working school acknowledged the important need of this by setting up a buddy system for all new SEN intakes. As pupils became more confident, support was withdrawn to allow dining hall independence.

- **If a pupil has difficulty in choosing where to sit or consistently chooses other challenging children to sit beside, designating a regular seat in the dining hall is useful.** *This should be 'safe', where they can be easily observed by staff and ensure that sympathetic and good behaviour role models are seated close by. Because individuals typically respond better to the visual rather than the verbal rule name labelling a younger child's chair can make this easier.*

Unfortunately, pupils with autism (especially those with AS who desperately want to join in) can easily be persuaded by those 'more challenging children' to sit next to them. As naughty behaviours of others escalate, the pupil with autism may become involved. One pupil, despite showing good behaviour at all other times, was often in trouble (as were the rest of his table) at lunchtimes. This frequently resulted in him being sent to sit on 'the naughty mat', or to eat his lunch in the Head Teacher's office. For a child who only ever wanted to 'join in' and naturally couldn't learn from his mistakes, this caused him great distress. When moved to a table with sympathetic and good role models, also being designated his own 'special chair' (in full view of supervisory assistants) the pupil was quickly settled into much happier lunchtimes. To help his association with the chair being 'special', supervisory staff encouraged him to help make a name label for it.

- **Pupils may have difficulty in understanding rules of the dining hall – both written and especially, the socially 'unwritten'.**
  Spending a few minutes going through written rules to discover the pupil's own understanding and interpretation of the rules is valuable. It also helps to discuss the 'unwritten' rules of expected behaviour. Using their own words and/or visual reminders helps pupils achieve a more precise understanding of expectations, so encouraging them to make their own reminder posters can be valuable.

School was experiencing difficulties with a pupil who, although he properly helped stack dining hall chairs, would then climb up onto the top of them (at one time, ten of them) and quietly sit there. After each time this happened, staff dutifully explained it was dangerous, that he might fall etc. Despite this, the pupil's climbing and sitting quickly extended into the classroom. For a child who *never* sat still on his chair during a lesson or lunchtime this seemed an extremely 'odd' thing to do. When later going through classroom rules with him I noticed that one of them was 'Sit on the chairs'. For an intelligent individual prone to literal interpretation and desperate to do the right thing, also one who responded much better to the visual rather than the verbal rule, he had merely been doing **exactly** as he had been told! The fact he had never fallen, despite being warned he 'might' do, was, because of his imagination skills impairment, of no useful deterrent at all. By teaching a good chair sitting technique – ie: one chair with all four legs on floor, bottom on chair, feet on floor, and amending the rule to the pupil's own (acceptable) version of this - 'Good sitting on my chair' - there were no further occurrences of earlier difficulties. To stress and reward the importance and understanding of this, the pupil was encouraged to make a poster reminder for the whole school, including the dining hall, to use. His final reward was a certificate in that week's assembly celebrating his 'Safety in School' sense.

- **School lunchtimes are naturally often very noisy. Some pupils find the noise level unbearable at times, either covering their ears or displaying their own self-comforting behaviours.** *Verbal acknowledgement of the noise level is often enough to reassure a pupil. Reminders of their own quiet table and space builds on this.*

It is easy for noise in the dining hall to escalate to extreme proportions un-noticed as it's actually happening. What usually eventually catches busy staff attention is the sound of the one pupil who, despite the horrendous overall din, can still clearly be heard above the rest. In many cases this will be a pupil with autism either desperately trying to regain some sense of control over the confusing and uncomfortable situation or simply, staff attention. A simple "Yes, it is noisy in here" followed by a reassuring "But look how quiet people at your table are being" was far more effective and honestly required than reprimanding a Yr 5 pupil with AS for his own loud but self-comforting reactions. Teaching him to put his hand up or cover his ears to signal it was too noisy for him provided him with more acceptable ways to ask staff for help.

- **Some pupils with autism (just like some without it) may need extra support to be able to use their cutlery and/or eat politely.** *Some may possess fine motor difficulties making it difficult to use eating and drinking tools. Depending on individual needs, socially acceptable dining skills may either require actual staff modelling, or visual pointers and reminders of how good role models in the immediate vicinity are behaving. If messy eating is a hugely obvious problem setting aside a screened 'special' table for staff directed group teaching may be most practical.*

Although originally called to address messy eating difficulties of a pupil with AS, one school with a high percentage of SEN children opted to set aside a screened area for supervised others to use as well. This had the added bonus of not singling the child out, and of staff being able to encourage other social skills as well. As eating habits and table manners improved, pupils (including the originally designated one) were re-introduced back into the main part of the dining hall. From time to time, and by way of reminding pupils of their achievements, they were called on to act as good role models for new participants, for which they were awarded stickers.

- **Awarding stickers for good behaviours can be extremely useful.** *However, any good behaviour may initially require teaching, modelling and/or exact verbal explanation. For some pupils this may even extend to the acquisition of good sitting and walking techniques. Targeting one or two specific behaviours each week for whole groups of children avoids singling an individual out. For optimum effect, stickers should be awarded immediately – ie. **Catching the pupil whilst being good.** Because some pupils may have an obsessive preference or interest for certain colours, objects, or TV characters etc – using related stickers provides even greater incentive to earning one.*

In the case of the pupil mentioned in the previous strategy, dinosaur stickers were used. Whilst most schools have access to sticker catalogues, many do not pass these on to (midday) supervisory staff. Ensuring all supervisors have access, also a small budget for these (specialist stickers – eg. Winnie the Pooh/Barbie/Tarzan can more often be found in supermarkets etc) is a good way of providing them with tangible, sought after rewards to use with pupils. Some schools have been further persuaded to support MSA's in their important role by allowing them to award weekly target behaviour certificates at the end of each week.

ASD specialist approaches in the playground

- **Pupils may not connect indoor/outdoor supervisors as being there to help in both settings.** *Reminders at the beginning of outdoor playtime sessions are useful. Also reminding pupils of where supervisory staff can be found should help be needed is also beneficial, particularly in secondary school settings.*

I go back now to the little boy who, desperate to use the toilet during lunch, ran out of the hall to find his teacher to ask permission, by which time it was too late. In this case, and although having been introduced to supervisory assistants *inside* the dining hall, he was also reminded them *outside*. This acknowledged the pupil's own lack of generalisation skills also often evident in other individuals.

Two of the most common complaints among secondary pupils about breaktimes (particularly outdoor ones) is not knowing who to approach, or where to find someone to approach for help. Most secondary schools have designated playground areas where supervisory staff usually stand. Physically pointing these out to pupils (supported by a simple plan) is an effective and easy way to inform of this. Buddy systems may be used to help with this.

These strategies worked particularly well with a student who had become increasingly reluctant to venture outside at break and lunchtimes. When discussing it with him, he revealed that the previous term he had been tripped up and become frightened but didn't know where to find help. Having been equipped to know where to find help should any other needy situations occur, initially buddy supported, the pupil happily resumed going outside at breaktimes.

- **If line up times are a problem (particularly with pushing etc of other children) staff may need to teach 'hands by your side' or 'folded in front of you' as acceptable body control alternatives.** *This kind of pushing may be an odd social approach so teaching a more polite tap on the shoulder instead could help. For those pupils with odd verbal displays, teach a more appropriate alternative such as "Excuse me", or even a simple "Hello". Pupils prone to literal interpretation or other associated language disorder may be confused when told to go (for example) to 'the back' of the line. Until understanding this has been learned staff may need to point or even physically guide the child to the correct place.*

25

A reception pupil was having difficulties at line up time, often pushing others or 'barging in' where he shouldn't have been. On the occasions he *was* joining the line up 'quietly', he was then either pulling other's hair or pinching their faces. Teaching the whole class a simple 'Hands by your side (and keep them there)' **after** the bell and **before** lining up was a simple and effective way of preventing opportunity for inappropriate physical approaches.

An older primary pupil, although quickly responding to the call for line up, then frequently approached those around him with odd verbalisations including 'I can fly'. This caused laughter or jibes from others, which, in turn, provoked the child into running out of line and around the playground, furiously flapping his arms. He then re-joined the line quietly. Acknowledging his need of verbal and physical cut off points to signal the end of outside playtime, staff were encouraged to offer him to repeat "I can line up quietly" instead. Simultaneous teaching of hands by your side stance reinforced this. Initially, and to further persuade him (and others) to continue in more acceptable line up behaviour, stickers were awarded.

- **Playtimes are generally recommended to be 'free' times for all children – including those with ASD. However, in extreme cases this can do more harm than good.** *For younger children, encouraging and directing simple small group games for a few minutes of outside playtime allows staff the opportunity to help develop social, conversational and friendship skills, and to boost pupil confidence and self-esteem. Older pupils frequently benefit from the provision of 'safer' alternate indoor location and activities.*

After an apparently good start in Yr 7, George's overall behaviour deteriorated so quickly and so badly that only two terms later it was decided he should attend mornings only. Where before George had happily played football outside he now sat alone, rocking and chanting, in the corner of the 'Safe room'. Supervisory staff, in the desperate hopes George might somehow 'gather himself' if left to his own devices, had continued to respect morning breaks (now his only real chance of socialising with others) as his free time.

With SENCO and parent agreement and support, supervisory staff began to start the slow but successful process of reintegrating George back into the safe room group. The starting point here was for a trusted member of supervisory staff (by trusted I mean one George had earlier formed – before his withdrawal - a good working relationship with) to initially encourage him in a 1-1 card game. To begin with this was for only a few minutes.

Initially allowing George to win the game provided him with a wholly positive memory of the experience. As supervisory staff daily persevered in this 1-1, George slowly became more confident within the 'Safe Room' environment. The gradual and discreet warning and introduction of others (staff and students) to the game always ensured George retained some sense of control. Having regained confidence and happiness during safe room breaktimes, the next part of the process was to begin slowly encouraging George to venture outside again (for football). This was initially staff supported with one other student and in a quiet area of the playground.

In George's case, and as may be required with other pupils in similar extreme situations, a multi-disciplinary approach may be required for optimum benefits.

- **Awarding immediate verbal praise, stickers or obvious 'thumbs up' for good behaviours in the playground is beneficial.** *However, these behaviours may need to be modelled etc first.*

Using a 'thumbs up' sign or verbal praise are both very useful when stickers aren't available or the breaktime quota has already been used. These simple strategies are particularly useful for catching the pupil when he or she is showing good behaviours in known areas of difficulty. For some pupils, 'being good' may initially be too fleeting to even allow the retrieval and physical award of a sticker!

- **If outside play is a particular problem, the pupil can be rewarded with computer or other preferred indoor activity afterwards.** *Depending on the child and staff resources this time can be taken alone or with another to further encourage sharing/turn taking/friendship skills etc. For maximum effect and co-operation, any reward like this should be given immediately – ie: 20 mins outside/20 mins inside. Staff may also consider regular timetabling of supervised indoor playtimes into weekly schedules.*

School was having difficulty in encouraging a pupil to outside play. By helping him adapt his timetable to show LUNCH, PLAYGROUND & COMPUTER times as opposed to just 'lunch' time, he was more easily persuaded to go outside (In this case, initially three times a week with 50/50 time split although these can be adapted according to individual needs and staff resource available).

- **Going through playground rules to find acceptable version in the pupil's own words is invaluable.** *Encouraging and allowing pupils to make poster reminders on the computer provides visual reinforcement of them. Later using individual pupil wording of playground rules ensures easier understanding and co-operation of them.*

After a particularly bad bout of aggressive playground behaviour from a pupil, staff helped him make a rules poster. Rules included 'No thumping', 'No pinching' and 'No hair pulling'. For a while, this strategy seemed to help and the child's behaviour improved. Some time later, and when reminded of his poster after he'd been seen thumping a child, the boy tearfully claimed he hadn't broken any of the rules, becoming extremely distressed with apparently no understanding of why he was in trouble. When later discussing this with him, I noticed the boy used the word 'punch' as well as 'thump'. When asked to show me how he did both, he tucked his thumb inside his clenched fist for the first, but kept it outside for the second. To him, there was a definite difference between them! Amending his rules to include both more fully equipped staff to manage his behaviour.

- **Some pupils harbour unhappy play/lunchtime experiences for long periods of time – this may extend to weeks and months - before eventually seeking their own, often untimely and inappropriate retribution.** *To find out what has happened in an individual session, instruct a pupil to tell of one good and then one bad thing, about it. If an upsetting incident has occurred this can then be quickly, and appropriately attended to. Some language impaired children may benefit from being encouraged to show a 'help' or 'something has upset me' card.*

After an apparently good term start, a pupil with AS suddenly began getting into trouble for being aggressive at playtimes. When questioned about this, each of the involved others remained adamant they had done nothing to encourage such behaviour from him. Staff and peer witnesses to each incident confirmed this. It was eventually discovered that all those children the pupil had been recently aggressive to had, but 'ages ago', either said or done something to upset him. Providing the pupil with regular opportunity to tell of individual play and breaktime experiences ensured there were no further similar displays from him.

28

- **Secondary school pupils may also benefit from an adapted system whereby they are encouraged to post a 'help' note on the SEN staff notice board.** *One way of introducing this is to describe it as 'giving the problem away' for someone else to deal with. Pupils should always be informed of the outcome of this - no matter how seemingly 'small' the problem – not only to boost confidence of having finally done the right thing, but also to encourage future use of the system.*

A particularly astute SENCO set this system up in her school to initially assist a rather nervous newcomer who was finding it increasingly difficult to distinguish between 'bullying' and 'accidental knocking into' during corridor, line up and break and lunchtimes. 'Giving the problem away' meant the pupil didn't feel he had to dwell on it as previously. Always informing him of the reality and outcome of a particular incident – ie. accidental or otherwise – slowly enabled the pupil to learn to distinguish between, and react more appropriately to a given situation. The added knowledge that any real bullying of him had been addressed provided further reassurance. Over a period of time the number of help notes from him decreased. On the rare occasion one did appear, it was usually discovered to be a bullying or teasing issue.

ASD specialist approaches for indoor playtimes

- **These naturally noisy, often 'last minute' chaotic sessions are typically difficult times for children with ASD.** *When left to their own devices, pupils commonly resort to individual self-comforting and inappropriate behaviours. These in themselves may lead to all sorts of connected problems particularly in such an enclosed and obvious, environment. Structuring and directing some indoor play and sharing time is frequently invaluable. Depending on the individual this can either be a few minutes of 1-1 or small group worked game followed by a limited choice of activities afterwards. Whilst most other children relish being able to choose from the vast array of toys, books and other activities on offer those with ASD often become confused when faced with this scenario. Limiting the choice to only one or two will greatly reduce pupil confusion.*

Despite having no problems during outside play, a primary pupil was frequently aggressive and disruptive during indoor play. By structuring his time to initially include a board game 1-1 with staff, then reading and computer time, his (and staff) frustrations soon disappeared. As his behaviour became calmer, other children and different activities were introduced, ultimately achieving his more inclusive, independent participation.

NB: When structuring indoor playtime for a pupil, supervisory staff should liase with classroom staff to ensure favourite games/activities are initially chosen. This makes it much easier to ensure the pupil's co-operation.

- **A pupil may twizzle or flap objects having little or no idea or regard of what they are actually for. Staff may need to teach how certain specific toys or tools are used.** *Some acceptable 'flapping/twizzling' time can be used as reward for other playtime participation first. NB: Whilst we should always acknowledge an individual's 'unusual' needs as being real ones, guiding them towards more 'socially appropriate' and therefore more acceptably inclusive activities, times and places, is perfectly reasonable. For those pupils who prefer to run up and down or around playground boundaries to use the hall for a few minutes or organising chasing/running games in small, sympathetic groups, can be beneficial during indoor playtimes.*

Whenever he became particularly stressed or just wanted to 'switch off', Steven would rip off a length of paper (it didn't matter where from) and flap it in front of his eyes. By initially using one minute of flapping time, but only *after* he'd joined in with a staff supervised game or activity first, and also providing him with a tray of 'flapping paper' and 'flapper bin', staff were gradually able to persuade and reward Steven's more inclusive, enjoyable and acceptable participation during indoor play. Acknowledging his real need of flapping, also providing Steven with suitable times and resources to do it ultimately resulted in decreased displays of it.

- **More fully inclusive schools recognise pupil needs for a safe and quiet haven or refuge to retreat to during times of unavoidable distress.** *For some, these may include indoor playtimes. Even knowing a safe place is available to use if needs be often works to decrease intensity and duration of pupil temper tantrums or displays of other 'inappropriate' self-comforting behaviours. Using screens and/or cushions for pupils to retreat to is the easiest way to provide quiet space. Ensuring the quiet space is made as otherwise 'uninteresting' as possible to the pupil works to avoid unnecessary extended or 'cunningly manipulated' misuse of it – as does consistently verbally or visually imposing given duration time. More inclusive secondary schools nowadays provide supervised 'safe' rooms for older pupils to retreat to.*

This strategy is an extension of one I originally saw being worked in a busy classroom environment. Whenever a particular task became too much for him, a pupil was allowed to retreat to an otherwise blank screened and cushioned area in the corner of the room – but only ever for a limited period of time – and always on the understanding he would have to finish his work afterwards. When later applied to include the difficulties he was experiencing during indoor playtime situations (poor sharing and turn-taking skills), his 'returning task' would be to finish the game or activity to conclusion. Initially providing him with three 'time out' cards to use during an entire playtime (one of which he had to give to staff before retreating to the screened area) not only limited his withdrawal time but provided him with a very visible, tangible 'indoor playtime rule' to adhere to. As he became more confident in his sharing and turn-taking skills, thereby more independently able to join in with others, his voluntary 'time outs' stopped.

- **Finally, whilst some schools acknowledge the importance of good home/school liaison relating to difficulties in the classroom, many**

more forget the relevance of extending this to include managing break and lunchtime behaviours. *Parents can often provide successful approaches they use at home during eating, playing and social times. If not entirely suitable for school use in present format, some of these approaches can be adapted accordingly. Also, some parents are willing to reinforce successful school approaches at home.*

Discussing break and lunchtime difficulties with parents may give an even better insight into why a pupil is behaving as he or she is during these times. Jayne, the little girl who apparently didn't like to tidy away, simply didn't have to at home. Frustrated by her previous attempts to encourage this, Mum had finally resorted to doing it all for her. By using the same techniques at home as at school, Jayne's parents were able to encourage and reinforce the importance of her participation during tidy times.

To reinforce the importance of good table manners at school, Mark's parents (the boy who 'choked') used an incentive of a McDonalds visit for him and a chosen friend as a reward.

When discussing Steven's paper flapping displays with his parents, they told that the bedroom he shared with his brother at home was often literally strewn with his flappers. Many of the flappers, much to his brother's upset, had been torn from his brother's comics. By providing Steven with back dated comics, also a 'flapper paper tray' and a 'flapper bin', his parents not only reinforced the technique school was using, but helped put a stop to the fights and arguments previously caused between Steven and his brother about this.

Experience proves that parents are frequently grateful for the opportunity to be included in more effective management of their child but, and just like MSA's, currently remain a vastly underused, underestimated resource. As is, of course, the pupil him or herself... *Although some older, more capable pupils may be invited to annual statement review meetings, experience proves that when specifically discussing break and lunchtime difficulties, pupils are often excluded.*

An effective way of discovering a pupil's own viewpoint on play and lunchtimes is to ask a series of simple questions, the most useful of which have briefly already been mentioned. ie. 'Tell me one good thing about play (and lunch) times', followed by 'Now tell me one bad thing' Answers to these give staff, without putting too much pressure on a pupil, a good starting point of information. Depending on a pupil's response to these, staff can then 'fine-tune' subsequent questions to suit each individual situation.

This type of 'scaffolding' strategy was used with the child who had 'punched' and not 'thumped'. The abridged version of relevant parts of the conversation went something like this:

Having answered, "I get into trouble" to the 'one bad thing' question, I then asked him to tell me of one way he gets into trouble. 'By fighting'.

Tell me one way you fight. 'By kicking'.

Tell me two more ways you fight. 'By punching and thumping'.

Show me, without doing it to me, how you punch ... *and so on.*

Conclusion

For most effective approaches to difficult break and lunchtime behaviours, supervisory staff must be prepared and provided with opportunity to work together with classroom staff, parents and pupils as opposed to remaining (as is so often currently the case) an independent, unknown body. More fully inclusive working schools acknowledge the need and importance of this.

Including pupils with Autism at break and lunchtimes

Afterword

Despite best efforts pupils may still display 'inappropriate' behaviour. However, before addressing *any* display of play or lunchtime behaviour as 'inappropriate' attending staff must first work to discover the true reason for it. ie. What did the individual ultimately achieve to placate him or her as a result of that behaviour? Was it an ASD affected communicative attempt at making friends, meeting real individual needs, responding to a certain situation and/or joining in? If so, staff should offer more widely understood, socially acceptable alternatives. Whatever emerges, spending a few considered moments distinguishing between 'autistic' and 'naughty' displays of pupil behaviour is undoubtedly a most effective and precious thing.